Introduction

Ever since I can remember, I have loved the smell of baking coming from my mom's oven and as a child, I always wanted to bake and create new things in the kitchen with her. That's why I bought a very expensive notebook and wrote down the simplest and most successful recipes. This notebook is still not full as I am very strict about what goes in it.

This book is a compilation of the recipes that I have collected in the past eighteen years. I have improved them, adapted them and substituted ingredients for milk-free alternatives.

The mixture of milk and meat is prohibited under Jewish law. In the Torah it is written: "You shall not boil a kid in his mother's milk" (Exodus 23:19). Not only must one not eat meat and milk in the same meal, one must wait a specific period of time before eating milk after eating meat. For that matter, if you eat a meaty main course, you will have to eat a non-dairy dessert.

Bon appétit!

*At the end of this book you will find alternative ingredients for dairy options.

ISBN: 978-965-92007-0-2

ACKNOWLEDGEMENTS:

I would like to thank everyone who contributed and helped me with this project. Without you I would not have been able to finish this book.

I would like to thank:

My mother, Shoshana Morhin – who has always supported my passion for cooking.

Revital Mor-Haim – who edited, designed and took photographs for this book perfectly with her creativity and diligence!

Ayelet Rabinovitch, who took photographs for this book. You have an extraordinary talent. Thanks for revealing your world to me.

Hunderwasser – Tali's shop for housewares

Special thanks to my husband, Doron Kettner, for all his love and support, which gave me the strength and encouragement to write and publish this book.

CONTENTS

BASIC SPONGE WITH FRUIT AND CREAM

Preparation time: 15min
Baking time: 30min

For the sponge:

5 eggs

5 tablespoons sugar

1 tablespoon brandy (optional)

5 heaped tablespoons flour

1 teaspoon baking powder

1 teaspoon vanilla extract

1 tablespoon oil

For the syrup:

If you use canned fruit, you can use the syrup from the can.

If you use fresh fruit, make the syrup:

1 cup water

1/2 cup sugar

1 teaspoon vanilla extract

Boil together and let cool

For decoration:

250ml non-dairy sweet cream, whipped

1 can of fruit (e.g. peach, apricot, pineapple)

1 jelly box (90 grams) to match chosen fruit

Method:

Mix the eggs at maximum speed, add sugar and when the mixture turns white and fluffy, slow the mixer and add the rest of the ingredients in order. Put in a 26 cm baking pan and bake for 30 minutes or until a toothpick inserted into the cake comes out dry. Leave the cake to cool.

For a larger cake add more eggs, sugar, and flour proportionally.

When the cake is cool, cut in half and use the syrup to wet the cake on both halves of the cake, and then put whipped cream on the base layer. Place the top layer of sponge on top of the cream. On the whole cake, arrange the fruit nicely and cover with the jelly. Make sure you get good coverage.

Cool in the fridge for 3 hours before eating.

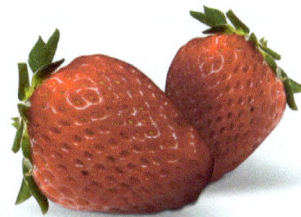

CARROT MUFFINS

Preparation time: 15min
Baking time: 45min

Ingridients:

3/4 cups sugar

1/4 cup oil

1 cup flour

1 teaspoon baking powder

1/4 teaspoon cinnamon

1/4 teaspoon nutmeg

2 eggs

1/4 cups walnuts

3/4 cup coarsely grated carrot

Method:

Mix all ingredients in a bowl, then pour them into a muffin tray to make 8 muffins or into one large loaf tin (24x7 cm or similar). Bake at 180°C for 30-45 minutes.
You can check with a toothpick, inserted into the cake - when it comes out dry the baking is done.

FINE FLOUR CAKE

Preparation time: 10min
Baking time: 40min

Ingridients:

5 eggs

1 cup sugar

1 cup canola oil

1 cup flour

1 cup fine flour

1 cup coconut chips

1 cup orange juice

1 teaspoon baking powder

1 teaspoon vanilla sugar

For the syrup:

2 cups sugar

1 cup water

Juice from half a lemon

Method:

Stir all ingredients to form a thick mixture.

Put in 26 cm baking pan and bake at 175ºC for 40 minutes.

While the cake is in the oven, make the syrup by heating all the ingredients until the sugar has melted. When the cake is ready (when a toothpick inserted into the cake and dry out), pour the syrup over it and then put in the oven for 15 minutes more.

For decoration, scatter coconut chips.

HONEY CAKE

Preparation time: 15min
Baking time: 45min

Ingridients:

2 cups flour	1 cup honey
2 teaspoons baking powder	1 cup sugar
2 tablespoons cocoa	1 cup boiling water
2 eggs	1/2 cup oil

Method:

Whip the eggs and sugar to make a light, creamy mixture. Add the sugar, honey, and oil. Gradually add the flour and whip on a slow setting. Then add baking powder and cocoa. Finally, add the boiling water. Bake at 175ºC for 45 minutes or until a toothpick inserted into the cake comes out dry.

Allow the cake to cool before dusting with powdered sugar.

APPLE HUT CAKE

Preparation time: 15min
Baking time: 45min

Ingridients:

4 apples

2 tablespoons cinnamon

3 tablespoons sweet wine/
2 tablespoons sugar

1 cup sugar

1/2 cup oil

3 eggs

2 cups flour

1 teaspoon baking powder

100 grams nuts

50 grams bitter chocolate/
raisins/cherries

Method:

Cut the apples into 1 cm cubes and cover with cinnamon and wine or sugar.

In another bowl, stir the eggs with sugar, add the oil, flour, and baking powder. Put in a 26 cm baking pan. On the mixture, put the retted apples and scatter fragments of nuts, and any other topping you like (Bitter chocolate/ raisings/ cherries).

Bake in 175°C until a toothpick inserted into the cake comes out dry.

Rivkale's Bakery

Dairy-Free recipes

APPLE PIE

Preparation time: 20min
Baking time: 1hour

For the pastry:

4 cups flour

200 grams margarine

1/2 cup orange juice or water

1 teaspoon baking powder

2 tablespoon sugar

For the filling:

8 apples, coarsely grated.

6 tablespoons sugar

3 teaspoons cinnamon

For decoration:

2 tablespoons oil

1 teaspoon cinnamon

2 tablespoons sugar

Method:

Mix all the ingredients together for the pastry. If necessary, add a little extra flour so the dough doesn't stick to your hands.

Divide the pastry dough in half. Roll out one half and put in the base of the pan, size 26cm.

Pour in the apple mixture and cover with the rest of the dough, making sure to seal the edges well. Spread the oil all over the cake and then sprinkle with cinnamon and sugar on the top of the cake. Put in the oven for 1 hour at 180°C.

APPLE CRUMBLE

Preparation time: 40min
Baking time: 40min

For the crumble:

1 cup sugar

3 cups flour

1 teaspoon baking powder

200 grams margarine

1 tablespoon water

For the filling:

6 sweet apples (any kind you like), grated medium thick

1/2 cup chopped nuts

4 tablespoons sugar

4 teaspoons cinnamon

Method:

Mix all ingredients of the cramble together, to make the dough.

Split the dough to 1/3 & 2/3.

Roll out 2/3 dough and put in the pan. Disperse half of the apples on the flattened dough and scatter 1/4 cup chopped nuts, 2 tablespoons sugar and 2 teaspoons cinnamon. Disperse the second half with the rest of nuts, sugar and cinnamon to create a second layer. Roll the remaining 1/3 dough into small balls in the size of raisins with your hands and spread them all over the cake. Alternatively, freeze the dough then grate into little pieces. Bake at 175°C until the crumble turns golden brown.

JAM PIE

Preparation time: 15min
Baking time: 40min

For the pastry:

100 grams margarine

1 1/4 cups flour

1 teaspoon baking powder

1 egg

1/4 cup sugar

For the filling:

1 jar of jam of any flavor
(300 grams)

Method:

Mix all the pastry ingredients together.

Divide the dough into 1/3 and 2/3. Take 2/3 part, roll out and place in the pan.

Put the jam on top of the dough. Then roll out the rest of the dough and cut long strips 1 cm wide. The dough stripes should be placed at a 2 cm distance from each other, both to the length and the width of the plate.

Bake at 170ºC until the top is golden brown.

BANANA CAKE WITH WHITE CHOCOLATE CHIPS

Preparation time: 10min
Baking time: 50min

Ingridients:

200 grams melted margarine

2 eggs

1/4 cup water

1 1/2 cups sugar

1/2 teaspoon salt

2 cups flour

1 teaspoon baking powder

4 ripe bananas, mashed

1/2 cup white chocolate chips (nondairy)

Method:

Mix all ingredients in a bowl and bake at 175°C until a toothpick inserted into the cake comes out dry. The quantities listed in this recipe will make 2 loaf tin (24x7cm or similar) cakes.

CHOCOLATE SOUFFLÉ

Preparation time: 15min
Baking time: 10min

Ingridients

100 grams bittersweet chocolate (nondairy)

25 grams margarine

2 eggs

3 tablespoons sweetened cocoa

1/2 cup powdered sugar

Method:

Preheat the oven to 200°C.

Melt the chocolate in a pan with the butter. Add the cocoa and mix well. Separate the eggs and mix the yolks into the chocolate mixture.

Whisk the eggs whites and powdered sugar together to form a fluffy mixture, and then fold into the chocolate mixture.

Grease four small dishes with oil and then sprinkle with powdered sugar. Pour in the mixture to the bake for 7-10 minutes, until a crust forms on top of each soufflé. The middle of the soufflé should be runny, so make sure to take the cake out in time.

*Serve with vanilla ice-cream (optional).

RICH CHOCOLATE CAKE

Preparation time: 15min
Baking time: 40min

Ingredients:

4 eggs

1/2 cup oil

1 cup coconut milk or water

1 1/2 cup flour

2 spoons baking powder

1 cup sugar

2 tablespoon cocoa powder

2 tablespoons sweetened cocoa powder

For the coating:

200 grams bittersweet chocolate (nondairy)

250 grams nondairy cream

Method:

Stir all the ingredients together in a bowl. Put in a 26cm pan and bake at 180°C until a toothpick inserted into the cake comes out dry.

For the chocolate coating, melt the chocolate and the cream in a small pot, but don't bring to the boil. When the cake is ready, pierce holes in the cake using a toothpick and pour the coating over the cake, allowing it to fill the holes.

Serve warm or at room temperature.

POPPY SEED CAKE

Preparation time: 20min
Baking time: 40min

Ingredients:

200 grams minced poppy seeds

1 cup red wine

4 large eggs

1 1/2 cups sugar

1 teaspoon vanilla extract

1/2 cup oil

1 cup coconut chips

1 cup flour

1 teaspoon baking powder

For the coating:

4 tablespoons cocoa

6 tablespoons sugar

10 tablespoons water

50 grams margarine

Method:

Boil the minced poppy seed with the wine and let cool.

In a different bowl beat the eggs with the sugar, once white and airy add in the rest of the ingredients in order. Then add the poppy seed mixture.

Bake at 180°C Degrees until a toothpick inserted into the cake comes out dry.

For the coating, melt the cocoa, sugar, and water together in a pan.
When boiling, add margarine and stir until melted, pour on the cake.

CHOCOLATE YEAST CAKE

Preparation time: 2hours
Baking time: 40min

For the pastry:

6 cups flour

4 eggs

4 tablespoon sugar

50 grams fresh yeast

200 grams margarine

3/4 cup water

For the filling:

1 teaspoon vanilla extract

2 cups sugar

1 1/4 cups cocoa powder

300 grams margarine in room temperature

For the coating:

1 egg

4 tablespoons water

4 tablespoons sugar

2 tablespoons wine or water

Method:

To make the dough, mix all the ingredients together and leave to rise for 1 hour
(to get good results, put the dough in the oven in 30°C). Divide the dough into 4.

To make the filling mix all ingredients together to a form unit, divide to 4 for each cake.

Put the filling as shown in the chart below – step by step.

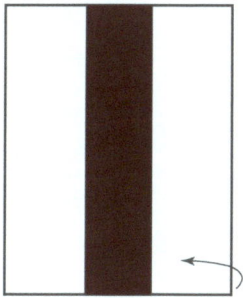

1 Smear some of the filling in the middle of the dough. Fold one side on the filling.

2 Smear more filling on one side of the doughand fold again until you get one long stripe.

3 On the long stripe smear filling in the middle and fold from bottom to the middle.

4 Put on the bottom side more filling and fold with the upper side.

5 Than you will have a folded rectangle.

6 Flatten the dough again to the original size as in section 1and pour the rest of the filling in the middle of the dough.On the sides, cut with a knife In diagonals as shown in the draw.

7 Take one diagonal from each side and put on each other every time from each side until you get a shape that looks like a braid.

Put each cake in a loaf baking pan and leave to rise for 30 minutes more.

brush with a beaten egg and Bake in the oven at 175°c until the cakes are brown.

While the cakes are in the oven, make the coating. Boil the water, sugar, and wine or water in a small pot and let cool until the sugar has melted. When the cake is ready and out the oven, cover the cake with the coating with a brash, for a glossy finish.

*the brown areas are where you should put the filling

CARROT MUFFINS Page 3

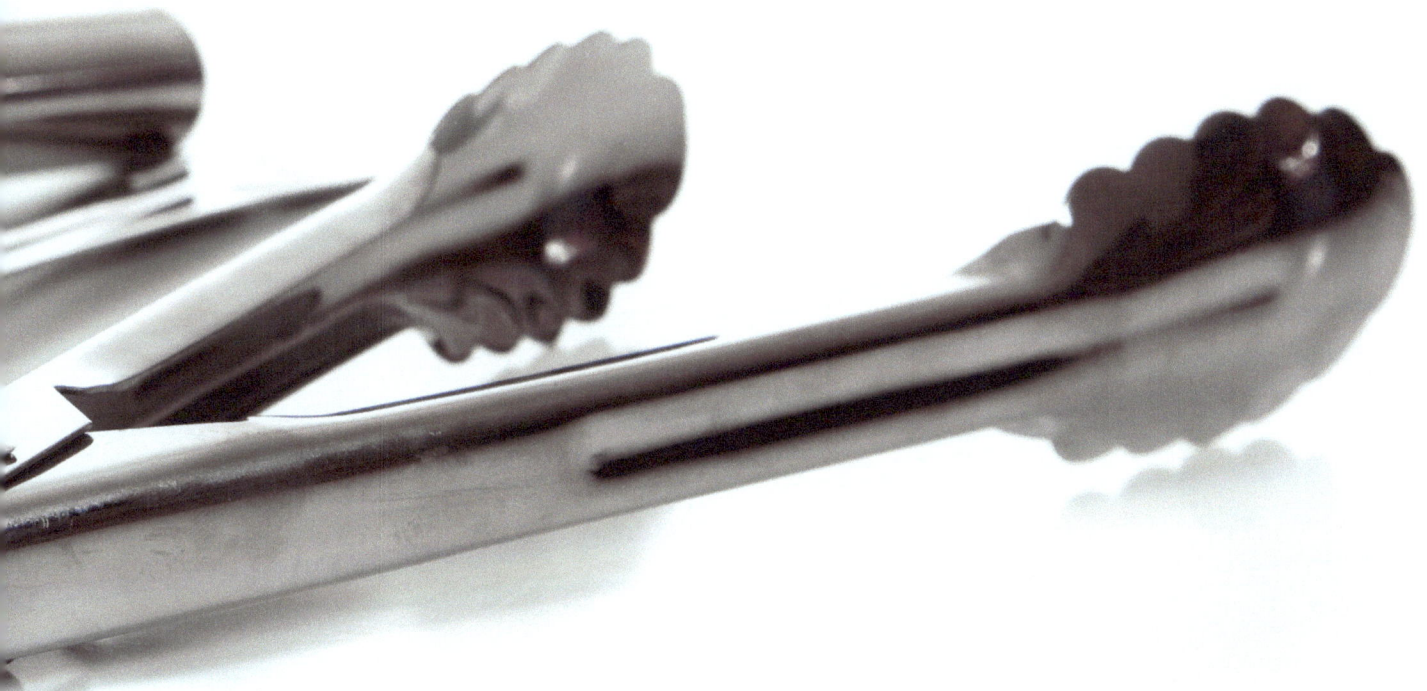

MOON COOKIES

Preparation time: 1hour
Baking time: 45min

Ingredients:

6 cups flour

2 eggs

1 cup sugar

300 grams margarine

6 tablespoons water

1 teaspoon baking powder

1 tablespoon lemon zest

A pinch of salt

Method:

Mix all ingredients together. Roll out the dough with your hands and create cookies in the shape of a half-moon. Take pieces of dough in the size of a Ping-Pong ball.

Make a form of a pipeline and then arch with your hands to a half-moon shape. Bake at 175°C for 30-45 minutes until the cookies are light brown.

For decoration, scatter powdered sugar when the cookies have cooled.

PALM ROLE

Preparation time: 30min
Baking time: 40min

For the pastry:

5 cups flour

1 teaspoon baking powder

1 teaspoon vanilla sugar

1/2 cup water

1/2 cup oil

200 grams butter flavored margarine

1/2 cup sugar

1 egg

For the Filling:

Grams date paste 450

10 teaspoons cinnamon

1 1/2 cup chopped nuts

Method:

Mix all the pastry ingredients together and leave to rest for 30 minutes. Then divide the dough into five equal pieces, to make 5 roles.

Take each piece and roll to a rectangle 30X15 cm. Spread 1/5 of the date paste onto each rolled out dough, sprinkle with 2 teaspoons cinnamon and 1/2 cup chopped nuts. Roll up the dough and mark slots every 2 cm.

Bake at 180°C for about 40 minutes until golden browning. When the roll is cold sprinkle it with powdered sugar.

SALTY COOKIES – PRETZELS

Preparation time: 1hour
Baking time: 40min

For the pastry:

3 cups flour

1 teaspoon baking powder

200 grams margarine

1/2 cup oil

1/2 teaspoon salt

1/2 cup water.

For the coating:

1/2 cup sesame seeds

1/2 cup cumin (optional)

1 egg

Method:

Mix all ingredients together to make the dough, but make sure to add in the water gradually. Create circles with a hole in the centre in a size of Ping-Pong ball per unit.

For the coating, fill one bowl with sesame and cumin seeds and in another, beat an egg. Dip the pretzel in the egg and then in the seeds.

Bake at 180°C until golden brown.

BUTTER FLAVORED COOKIES

Preparation time: 30min
Baking time: 40min

Ingredients:

cup powdered sugar

1/2 cup sugar

5 cups flour

400 grams margarine in butter flavor

1/2 cup oil

200 grams chopped walnuts

Method:

Mix all the ingredients to a form sticky dough mixture. With wet hands, roll into balls and flatten to make circles with a 5cm diameter. Place in the oven and bake at 180° until the cookies are very light golden brown.

For decoration, scatter powdered sugar when the cookies are cool.

PUMPKIN, SUNFLOWER & SESAME SEED COOKIES

Preparation time: 10min
Baking time: 15min

Ingredients:

200 grams sunflower seeds   1/2 cup brown sugar

200 grams pumpkin seeds   2 egg whites

100 grams sesame seeds

Method:

Stir all the ingredients together. With two teaspoons make balls and place them in a pan. Bake at 175°C for 15 minutes or until the bottom of the cookies are light brown.

Photography: Revital Mor-Haim

HAMANTASCHEN

Preparation time: 1hour
Baking time: 40min

For the cookie pastry see recipe for moon cookies on page 30
For the poppy seed filling:

1 cup sugar

1 cup water

200 grams minced poppy seeds

2 tablespoons lemon zest

2 teaspoons lemon juice

1 cup breadcrumbs

Method:

For the filling, heat the sugar and water, then add the poppy seeds and cook to a solid mixture (about 5 minutes). Add the lemon zest and lemon juice. Mix well and let cool.

To make the hamantaschen, roll out the dough until its 0.5 cm thick and then cut out circles with a small glass. Put a teaspoon of the poppy seed mixture in the center of the circle and fold the sides in to make a triangle shape.

Make sure you close the dough well, or else it might open when baking.

Bake at 180°C until the cookies very light brown then leave to cool.

For decoration, sprinkle cookies with powdered sugar.

YOYO

Preparation time: 1 hour

For the pastry:

2 eggs

4 tablespoons sugar

4 tablespoons oil

1 teaspoon baking powder

1 tablespoon vanilla sugar

2 1/2 cups flour

For Syrup 1:

1 cup sugar

1 cup water

For Syrup 2:

1 cup sugar

1 cup water

1/2 squeezed lemon

1 orange zest

1/2 teaspoon Cinnamon

Method:

Stir all ingredients to make pastry. Make 5cm round cookies with holes.

In the meantime make 2 syrups:

Syrup 1: Boil ingredients together in a pan and let cool

Syrup 2: Boil ingredients together in a pan and let cool

After the pastry and syrups have been prepared, fry the circles of dough. Make sure the oil in the pan is boiling. (I recommend boiling the oil on a high flame, and after adding the Yo-Yos, lowering it). They will swell immediately and will turn brown. Turn them over to brown the other side. Immediately after removing the Yo-Yos, pour in the syrup 1 for 3 seconds, and then syrup 2 for 3 more seconds. Then you can place the Yo-Yos on a plate. Serve in room temperature.

Conversion table from Nondairy to Dairy:

Non-Dairy	Dairy
200 grams margarine / 1/2 cup canola oil	200 grams butter
1 cup water juice / water / wine	1 cup milk
250grams coconut milk	250 grams dairy free cream
100 grams non-dairy bittersweet chocolate	100 grams milk chocolate

www.ingramcontent.com/pod-product-compliance
Lightning Source LLC
Chambersburg PA
CBHW042117040426

42449CB00002B/72